AF584434

World Heritage Sites in Australia

Port Arthur, Norfolk Island, Tasmanian Wilderness and more...

Tasmania and Australian Territories

Ellen Millen

First published 2017 by
Redback Publishing
PO Box 357 Frenchs Forest NSW 2086
Australia

978-1-925630-14-5

Author: Ellen Millen
Editor: Jane Hinchey
Designer: Redback Publishing

Original illustrations © Redback Publishing 2017
Originated by Redback Publishing

Printed and bound in China by Leo Paper

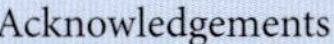

Acknowledgements
Abbreviations: l—left, r—right, b—bottom, t—top, c—centre, m—middle
We would like to thank the following for permission to reproduce photographs: (Images © shutterstock) p5b Hung Chung Chih, p23t Benny Marty, p23b Benny Marty, p25 By Barrylb (Own work) [CC0], via Wikimedia Commons ,p27t By JJ Harrison (jjharrison89@facebook.com) (Own work) [CC BY-SA 3.0 (http://creativecommons.org/licenses/by-sa/3.0)], via Wikimedia Commons, p30 By Astronaut photograph ISS018-E-38182 was acquired on February 28, 2009, with a Nikon D2Xs digital camera fitted with an 800 mm lens, and is provided by the ISS Crew Earth Observations experiment and the Image Science & Analysis Laboratory, Johnson Space Center. The image was taken by the Expedition 18 crew. The image in this article has been cropped and enhanced to improve contrast. Lens artifacts have been removed. The International Space Station Program supports the laboratory to help astronauts take pictures of Earth that will be of the greatest value to scientists and the public, and to make those images freely available on the Internet. Additional images taken by astronauts and cosmonauts can be viewed at the NASA/JSC Gateway to Astronaut Photography of Earth. Caption William L. Stefanov, NASA-JSC. [Public domain], via Wikimedia Commons

Every effort has been made to contact copyright holders of any material reproduced in this book. Any omissions will be rectified in subsequent printings if notice is given to the publisher.

Contents

What Makes a Place Special?

All around the world, people show that they value special places in different ways. Sites that are special because of their history, beauty or spiritual significance are preserved so that they do not deteriorate and will still exist for future generations to enjoy. Special places can be important for just one person, a group or community, or for everyone in the world.

Various groups in communities look after their special places in different ways

UNESCO

UNESCO identifies World Heritage places around the world.

Governments

Governments at all three levels in Australia make laws and regulations to identify, preserve and protect special places.

Community Groups

People in a local area often join together in groups to protect special places from destruction. Protest groups in Australia have been successful in the past in helping to preserve places of natural and built heritage. Many people donate their time and skills to help maintain special places such as bushland sites or historic buildings.

Individuals

Individuals who care about special places can look after them by being careful not to do anything that might degrade a site. Avoiding littering, not lighting campfires in the bush on days of high fire danger, and not engaging in graffiti or other unlawful activities all help to preserve special places.

Special Places

Make your own list of special places. The list could include homes, shops, parks or even a room or a special spot underneath a tree.

- Why are these places special to you?
- Will they still be important to you in the future?
- Are your special places important to anyone else?

Think about the places that are important just for you. Are they the same places that your friends or family think are special? What makes a place special to you?

World Heritage Sites and UNESCO

UNESCO is a division of the United Nations. It assesses sites around the world for their cultural and natural value to humanity. In 2017, there were 1,052 World Heritage Sites worldwide. Nineteen of these are in Australia.

> *"To be included on the World Heritage List, sites must be of outstanding universal value and meet at least one out of ten selection criteria"*

World Heritage Convention

The work on cataloguing World Heritage Sites began in 1972 as a result of an international treaty known as the World Heritage Convention. Australia was one of the first nations to become involved. Once a World Heritage Site has been determined, the country in which it exists must preserve and protect that site. Countries which have signed the treaty can work together to preserve sites that are of international importance.

World Heritage Committee

The World Heritage Committee is a group of some of the member countries of the United Nations. Committee members serve a fixed term. The role of this committee is to administer all matters relating to World Heritage Sites listings. Australia has been a committee member on a number of occasions.

UNESCO's World Heritage Mission

- To encourage more countries to sign the World Heritage Convention and contribute sites.
- To encourage countries to set up management plans for their sites.
- To provide emergency and technical assistance.
- To encourage local populations to become involved in preserving sites.

Threats to UNESCO World Heritage Sites

World Heritage Sites that are in danger of destruction are listed by UNESCO in their List of World Heritage in Danger. None of the sites in Australia are currently on this list. This is due to the diligent work undertaken by governments and individuals in Australia, and the high regard that Australians have for their heritage sites.

Threats to sites on the List of World Heritage in Danger currently include:

- Natural disasters like earthquakes or cyclones
- Wars and civil conflict
- Uncontrolled expansion of towns and cities
- Unchecked tourist development
- Neglect
- Lack of funds
- Pollution
- Poaching

In 2017, there were 55 sites listed by UNESCO as being under threat.

Bali, Indonesia

Statue of Liberty, USA

World Heritage Fund

Member nations contribute to the World Heritage Fund. Countries that do not have the financial resources to care for a site can apply for funding to assist them.

Redwood National and State Parks, USA

Hoi, Vietnam

Saving World Heritage Sites

UNESCO has been involved in saving some of the world's most iconic sites and their surroundings, including:

- Angkor, Cambodia
- Dubrovnik, Croatia
- Giza Pyramids, Egypt
- Delphi, Greece
- Abu Simbel, Egypt
- Venice, Italy

What is a Plan of Action?

Before setting out to protect a heritage site, it is important to have a Plan of Action. This plan will help to make the conservation process efficient and therefore more effective. Whether the heritage site or special place is being cared for by a government, a community group or an individual, their Plan of Action can include the following points:

- Set a definite goal.
- List the things that may stop this goal being achieved. Examples are a lack of funds, unfavourable weather or groups which oppose the goal.
- List all the activities that will be required to achieve the goal.
- Set priorities for which activities are the most important.
- Decide who will do the work required to achieve the goal.
- How will the goal affect other people who are not involved?
- Where will the funding come from?
- Work out a timetable for achieving the goal.
- Have regular reviews of the Plan of Action and make changes to it if necessary.

How a Heritage Listing Affects Communities

When a place receives a heritage listing, either from UNESCO, a government body or a private organisation, the listing can result in both positive and negative impacts on the community.

Positive Effects

- The heritage site is preserved for future generations.
- Owners of heritage listed buildings can apply for grants to help maintain them.
- Nations can apply for funding from UNESCO to care for their World Heritage Sites.
- More people know that the site exists.
- The world community can encourage nations to continue preserving their sites.
- Heritage sites produce a positive economic effect through their impact on tourism.

Negative Effects

- Indigenous people living in the area may be stopped from using it as a food source and as a place to perform traditional ceremonies.
- People may be stopped from using land as a holiday campsite.
- People cannot usually take pets with them into natural heritage areas.
- Farmers who have been grazing livestock in an area may be stopped from doing this.
- Houses that receive a heritage listing cannot be demolished or changed. Owners need special permits for any work on their building.
- Access to some areas in natural heritage sites may be restricted.
- The construction of roads and buildings is either not allowed or restricted.

Sustainable Tourism in World Heritage Sites

Tourism is a significant activity in World Heritage Sites. UNESCO advises countries with World Heritage Sites on sustainable ways to manage tourism.

At Australian World Heritage Sites, sustainable management of tourism includes:

- Building boardwalks or raised viewing platforms in natural areas so that tourists do not damage the environment when walking through it
- Closing sites, allowing them to regenerate
- Controlling the provision of sewerage and garbage services
- Restricting or forbidding access to sensitive areas
- Banning pets
- Educating the public on the value of the sites and how to behave when visiting them

Sustainability and World Heritage Sites

- Natural sites are involved in carbon storage in the form of trees and plants.
- Natural sites contribute to the water cycle and to climate regulation.
- Natural sites contribute to maintaining the Earth's biodiversity. This is important for the health of humanity, since many of our new medicines come from research undertaken into the properties of rare plants.
- UNESCO reports that climate change is likely to affect World Heritage Sites.

Q&A

Q. Can a place ever stop being a World Heritage Site?
A. Yes. The Arabian Oryx Sanctuary in Oman and the Elbe Valley in Dresden are no longer listed after failing to meet the requirements for preservation of the sites.

Mount Field National Park, Tasmania

Heritage Organisations in Australia

The Role of Governments and Heritage Councils

UNESCO is not the only organisation that determines whether places have heritage significance. The three levels of government in Australia, federal, state and local, also compile their own listings of important places. There are many more sites and items on these lists than on the World Heritage List for Australian places. Each state and territory has a Heritage Council which advises government on matters relating to heritage places.

Historic Shipwrecks Program

Shipwrecks more than 75 years old are protected by legislation. No items can be taken from them and divers must not move any part of the ship. Severe penalties apply. Shipwrecks that contain the remains of people, unexploded ammunition on warships or other sensitive contents may have access to them restricted. Anyone who discovers an historic shipwreck must report it to the government department responsible for shipwrecks in the relevant state.

Famous Australian Shipwrecks

- HMS Sirius in Slaughter Bay, Norfolk Island is one of the ships of the First Fleet
- Japanese midget submarine M24 from the Second World War is in the sea off Sydney

Overseas Special Places For Australia Listing

This listing is created by the Australian government.

- ANZAC Cove, Gallipoli
- Kokoda Track, Papua New Guinea
- Howard Florey's Laboratory, Sir William Dunn School of Pathology, UK

National Trust

The National Trust has organisations in each state and territory. Their aim is to preserve and promote Australia's cultural heritage. The National Trusts own over 300 heritage places.

Australian Institute of Architects

The Australian Institute of Architects keeps a list of notable buildings of cultural heritage across Australia. A building's importance is based on its aesthetic, historic, social, spiritual or technical value to the community.

Heritage Homework

Some school buildings around Australia are listed on state heritage registers. Is your school one of them? Are there any heritage listed school buildings in your area?

ANZAC Cove
Shipwreck

Australia's 19 World Heritage Properties (2017)

1. Australian Convict Sites
2. Australian Fossil Mammal Sites (Riversleigh / Naracoorte)
3. Fraser Island
4. Gondwana Rainforests of Australia
5. Great Barrier Reef
6. Greater Blue Mountains Area
7. Heard and McDonald Islands
8. Kakadu National Park
9. Lord Howe Island Group
10. Macquarie Island
11. Ningaloo Coast
12. Purnululu National Park
13. Royal Exhibition Building and Carlton Gardens
14. Shark Bay, Western Australia
15. Sydney Opera House
16. Tasmanian Wilderness
17. Uluru-Kata Tjuta National Park
18. Wet Tropics of Queensland
19. Willandra Lakes Region

Sydney Opera House

Blue Mountains
All World Heritage Sites in Australia are protected by law under the Environment Protection and Biodiversity Conservation Act 1999.
Purnululu National Park
Great Barrier Reef, QLD

Tasmanian Wilderness

The Tasmanian Wilderness was listed as a World Heritage Site in 1982. It covers 1.58 million hectares, which is about a fifth of the state. The wilderness protects examples of flora and fauna that are now extinct on the mainland of Australia, and is one of the last temperate rainforests left on Earth. It also contains significant Aboriginal sites that provide examples of how hunters and gatherers lived, and how people survived during extreme climatic conditions. The Tasmanian Wilderness is managed by the Parks and Wildlife Service of Tasmania.

Plants and Animals of the World Heritage Site

The protected wilderness of Tasmania has a range of environments, including moorlands, ancient pine forests, temperate rainforests, and both coastal and alpine areas. Some of the plants are descendants of species that have been growing there for millions of years, since the time when Tasmania was a part of the ancient continent of Gondwana.

There are extensive cave systems included in the heritage area. The Marakoopa Cave is open to the public and contains deposits from the last Ice-Age, as well as fascinating cave fauna, such as glow worms and the Tasmanian cave spider.

The majority of the animal species of Tasmania live within this World Heritage wilderness area. Some animals, such as the moss froglet, eastern quoll and Tasmanian pademelon probably do not exist anywhere else.

Cultural Heritage

The Tasmanian Wilderness was selected for both its natural features and its cultural importance. One of the sites that archaeologists have investigated is the Kutikina Cave. The rock art, tools and remains of human habitation found there, show that Aboriginal people lived in the cave up to 30,000 years ago. This included periods during the last Ice-Age when the climate was much colder than today. The Aboriginal people in Tasmania at that time were possibly the only people living so far south in the whole world.

Where is the Tasmanian Wilderness World Heritage Area?

There are a number of national parks and reserves that make up the Tasmanian Wilderness:

- Central Plateau Conservation Area
- Cradle Mountain-Lake St Claire
- Devils Gullet State Reserve
- Hartz Mountains
- Liffey Falls State Reserve
- Mole Creek Karst National Park
- Southwest National Park
- Walls of Jerusalem National Park
- Wild Rivers National Park

Threats to the Tasmanian Wilderness World Heritage Area

The Parks and Wildlife Service has identified the following threats to the Tasmanian Wilderness and has produced action plans to deal with them:

- Drought and climate change
- Fire
- Illegal activities such as logging or hunting
- Devil facial tumour disease in Tasmanian devils
- Plant diseases
- Weeds
- Pest animals
- Impacts from tourism
- Building of new structures
- Erosion along the coast
- Preservation of Aboriginal heritage
- The effects of hydroelectric power developments

Wild Rivers National Park

How the Tasmanian Wilderness is Protected

- No commercial logging is allowed.
- No mining is allowed.
- Aboriginal cultural heritage is maintained, including both sites and cultural practices.
- Places that were once used by settlers for mines, roads and dwellings have been rehabilitated.
- Sustainable access to the wilderness results in tourists causing minimal damage.
- Historic heritage is conserved, even though it is not included in the World Heritage listing.

Cradle Mountain

Think About It

Why doesn't the UNESCO World Heritage listing for the Tasmanian Wilderness include historic sites left by colonial settlers?

How the Tasmanian Wilderness World Heritage Listing Affects the Community

- Tourism to the Tasmanian Wilderness is important to Tasmania's economy.
- The cultural heritage of the traditional Aboriginal custodians is protected under the World Heritage listing.
- People who had farms in the wilderness before it was officially listed now have restrictions on their activities.

Environmental Campaigns

Cradle Mountain-Lake St Clair National Park

Lake Pedder, which is located in this park, was the focus of a conservation campaign by environmentalists in the 1960s.

Franklin and Gordon Rivers

In the 1980s, people who were concerned about damage to the wilderness opposed the proposed damming of the Franklin and Gordon Rivers. This campaign galvanised the green movement in Australia, which saw the birth of the Australian Greens Party.

Macquarie Island, TAS

Macquarie Island is a remote wilderness area, with a rugged and beautiful coastline. It is located in the Southern Ocean between Tasmania and the Antarctic.

There are two reasons Macquarie Island was listed as a World Heritage Site in 1997:

1. The only place on Earth where rocks from the mantle can be seen exposed above sea-level. The mantle rocks are usually six kilometres below the sea floor. Their exposure on Macquarie Island makes this place very interesting for geologists. The island is still geologically active, experiencing earthquakes as a result of the tectonic plate movements beneath it.

2. The island is a breeding site for extremely large numbers of penguins and seals. The Royal Penguins use Macquarie Island as their home base.

How Human Activity Has Changed Macquarie Island

Before Macquarie Island was listed as a heritage site, sealers killed seals for their fur and to make oil. Feral cats, the weka bird from New Zealand, rabbits, rats and mice were brought to the island, some on purpose and others as stowaways on ships. The Macquarie Island Pest Eradication Program has managed to rid the island of all these animals. The result has been that native vegetation is regrowing and the native birds no longer have their eggs and chicks eaten by rats.

Tourism

Tourism is tightly controlled and only 1,000 tourists are allowed to visit the island each year. Ships carrying more than 200 people are not allowed within the heritage site boundaries. Helicopters are not normally permitted to land.

Australian Antarctic Division (AAD)

The AAD base on Macquarie Island provides facilities for scientists to study the geology, climate and wildlife.

Australian Convict Sites

Why Are the Convict Sites Important?

Australia was founded as a convict colony, a place where Britain could send its thousands of prisoners. Convicted for a variety of crimes, including theft, assault or causing political disturbances, the convicts provided the labour which allowed Australia to grow into a bustling colony of Britain. They included women, men and children from the age of nine years old. The last convicts arrived in 1868, ending 80 years of transportation. Australia has eleven early convict World Heritage Sites.

What Do the Convict Sites Reveal About the Past?

- The types of housing people lived in.
- The difference in housing and places of work of different classes of people.
- The harshness of the punishments for criminals.
- Many jobs that once existed are now replaced by technological inventions.
- Technology has replaced domestic animals in transport and for ploughing fields.
- The daily life of convicts' children was very different from that of children today.
- We can observe how some building methods have not changed very much at all.

World Heritage Convict Sites in Tasmania

1. Port Arthur, TAS

Port Arthur was built as a prison to house convicts who had committed further crimes after arriving in the colony. Located on the lands of the Pydairrerme Aboriginal people, Port Arthur is now one of Tasmania's most important historic sites and a tourist attraction. The numerous buildings and extensive grounds present a picturesque vista for visitors and provide an insight into early colonial lifestyles.

From 1830 to 1877, Port Arthur was a place of punishment and misery. Convicts at Port Arthur experienced harsh conditions and hard labour while they were there. They worked in many trades and industries, including shipbuilding, logging, brick making and metal work. Any unacceptable behaviour was punished with flogging and solitary confinement.

Political prisoners from Ireland, Wales and Canada were also imprisoned at Port Arthur. They were separated from prisoners on the Australian mainland to stop them spreading anti-British views.

In 1834, Point Puer was established across the harbour from Port Arthur as a separate prison for convict boys from as young as nine years old. It was the first prison for boys in the British Empire, and was notorious for its harsh conditions.

Study of Port Arthur's past reveals information on the way people lived and thought during the colonial era, including:

- changing attitudes to the punishment of criminals
- changing attitudes to heritage conservation
- design and technology in the 1800s
- social history from the 1800s

Management Plan

Port Arthur has a formal management plan which guides the way the heritage site is used and conserved. Some of the points covered in this plan are:

- **Tourism:** Visitors are encouraged and facilities are provided for them.
- **Preservation:** The site is preserved and restored to keep its 19th century style intact.
- **Community:** Local residents are involved in the conservation plan.
- **Conflicts:** Management of the conflicting goals of allowing tourists access and preserving the site from damage.
- **Natural Threats:** Weathering is one of the main threats to the structures of Port Arthur. Dealing with the destructive effects of wind, rain and insect pests is a constant challenge.

2. Coal Mines Historic Site, TAS

This site on the Tasman Peninsula, near Saltwater River, was the location of Tasmania's first coal mine. Convict labour was used to mine coal so that Tasmania did not have to rely on importing it by ship from New South Wales. For over forty years, male convicts laboured at the mine and lived in miserable conditions. Their rows of stone cells are now in ruins but visitors can still imagine the lifestyle that the convicts endured. The chapel and bakehouse are reminders that even convicts had to eat and sought spiritual comfort.

Convict men who committed further crimes after they arrived in the colonies were sent to the Coal Mines for a punishment regime which was severe and relentless. Up to 500 convicts lived and worked at the site at any one time.

The Coal Mines Historic Site is a reminder that punishment for their crimes was only one reason thousands of convicts were sent to Australia. They were also needed to provide unpaid labour in a country that is very large and had a tiny population at the time.

History of Technology at the Coal Mines Historic Site

As well as the coal mining pits, the site also has the remains of a quarry, lime kilns that produced ingredients for mortar used in building, a tannery, wharves and many other associated stone structures. Although the site is in ruins, historians and archaeologists can study the way the coal was mined and transported, and compare that with the industrial technology of coal mining today.

Management of the Coal Mines Historic Site

The Coal Mines Historic Site is located on the Tasman Peninsula, near Premaydena. The Tasmanian Parks and Wildlife Service manages the site and restricts activities that could damage the remains.

Visitors should follow these directions:

- Supervise children
- Stay within barriers
- Beware of the deep mining shafts
- Do not take pets, metal detectors or firearms to the site
- Bicycle only on roads
- Do not disturb any building remnants

Think About It

Do you think these rules are necessary? What could happen if visitors ignored the rules?

3. Cascades Female Factory, TAS

Located outside Hobart, the Cascades Female Factory housed female convicts from 1828 until 1856. The accommodation included convict dormitories, solitary cells, a nursery, hospital and chapel. Female convicts sent to other British colonies in the early 1800s mostly became servants, and did not spend time in a prison. Australia's female factory system was unique.

The buildings at the Cascades Female Factory were both home and prison for thousands of women convicts. They waited there until they were assigned as servants to settlers, or they stayed there if they were too sick to work.

Convicts' Children

The women convicts sometimes had their children with them in the Cascades Female Factory, and there was a separate nursery area for women with babies. Studying this heritage site shows us the way people in the past treated children differently depending on whether their parents were convicts or free settlers. By 1838, over 200 babies had died at the site due to disease and poor living conditions. When the children were about two years old they were taken away to one of the orphanages.

Truganini

Truganini is the most well-known Aboriginal person in Tasmanian history. Although she is often called the last surviving Aboriginal person in the state, this is not correct, and many other Tasmanian Aboriginal people have descendants living today.

When Truganini died in 1876, her remains were buried in front of the chapel of the Cascades Female Factory. Her skeleton was later removed and put on display at the Hobart Museum. It was not until 1976, 100 years after her death, that Truganini's remains received a traditional burial.

Management of the Heritage Site

The Cascades Female Factory was sold in 1904 and many of the buildings were demolished. The value of heritage sites has changed over the years and they are now much more important to the community than they were in the past.

There are two aspects to the current management of this heritage site:

1. Preservation and restoration of the structures.
2. Managing and promoting tourist access.

4. Darlington Probation Station, TAS

Darlington Probation Station on Maria Island, off the east coast of Tasmania, was used as a prison for male convicts from 1842 until it closed in 1850. The location on Maria Island was chosen because its remoteness made escape less likely. It is the most intact prison of its type in Australia.

The convicts sent to the colonies were originally forced to work for settlers or the government. Their free labour was important for the economic growth of the colonies. In later years, the probation system was introduced to control them more strictly. This system divided prisoners according to their level of offence, and it was supposed to encourage them to reform. The convicts were divided into three classes, each one with different living conditions and privileges. All of this meant that special prisons had to be built. The Darlington Probation Station was one of these prisons.

The school room and chapel are reminders of the role of the probation system in reforming the inmates, while the solitary confinement cells show us that ongoing punishment was also imposed.

5. Brickendon and Woolmers Estates (near Longford, TAS)

The Brickendon Estate and the neighbouring Woolmers Estate have been preserved as examples of early homesteads in Tasmania. Visitors can see how important convict labour was to the running of a large household and farm in the 1800s. Together, these two homesteads form a rare example of a preserved colonial village in Australia.

The numerous outbuildings show the working and living conditions of the convict labourers, their separation from the free settlers, and the differing roles of male and female prisoners. The women worked around the house and slept in the attics, while the men worked outdoors and slept in the barracks.

The estates are full of examples of early technology, tools, kitchen and farm implements. Visitors can imagine what it was like to live there nearly 200 years ago when there was no electricity or modern machinery.

Management of the Heritage Site

The Brickendon and Woolmers Estates have been working farms since the 1820s, and this continuous use has contributed to their preservation. Some buildings have been turned into attractive tourist accommodation and others offer venues for functions such as weddings.

Think About This

What might have happened to farms in the 1800s if there had been no convicts to do the work needed to keep them functioning?

Darlington Probation Station

Convict Buildings, Brickendon Estate

Convict Buildings, Brickendon Estate

World Heritage Convict Site on Norfolk Island

Kingston and Arthurs Vale Historic Area

This historic site has World Heritage Value for a number of reasons:

- It was a convict site from 1788 until 1855. Changes in the treatment of convict prisoners over the years resulted in different ways of housing them. Examples of these changes can be seen in the buildings and archaeological remains on Norfolk Island.
- It is the only place in Australia where there was early settlement by Polynesian people, although none of them were left by the time the British arrived.
- The descendants of the mutineers from the ship, the Bounty, and their Tahitian wives, were resettled on Norfolk Island after being removed from Pitcairn Island in 1856.

Norfolk Island was a place where convicts endured brutal punishments. Its role as a prison was to deter people from committing crimes, by making them fearful about what would happen to them after being sent there. Norfolk Island had such a bad reputation that stories about the harsh conditions were used to support the movement in Britain against the transportation of convicts.

The Pitcairners

The Pitcairn Island descendants of the Bounty mutineers make up nearly one third of the population on Norfolk Island. They have developed a distinctive culture since their resettlement on the island in 1856. Their language and lifestyle have heritage importance as examples of the blending of Polynesian and European influences that has occurred on an isolated island over the past 160 years.

The Buildings

Norfolk Island's buildings dating from the 1820s onwards are a treasure trove for archaeologists and historians studying Australia's convict past. The remains of the places where the convicts worked reveal the differences between the technology used in the convict era and today. Without the benefit of modern machinery, all the hard labour was done by the convicts.

Connection with Sydney

Norfolk Island was claimed and settled by the British only six weeks after the town of Sydney was founded in 1788. While most of the early buildings of Sydney have been replaced with modern skyscrapers, many of the earliest buildings on Norfolk Island are still standing.

Australian Territories
Heard and Mcdonald Islands

Heard and McDonald Islands are Australian external territories located in the Southern Ocean, closer to Antarctica than to Australia. They are remote, wild and surrounded by dangerous waters. The islands are difficult to reach and inhospitable for humans. This has contributed to their pristine condition. They received a World Heritage Listing in 1997.

Reasons for the World Heritage Listing

- Completely undamaged ecosystems, with no introduced animals or plants and minimal human interference.
- The untouched location has allowed plants and animals on the islands to evolve naturally.
- The only volcanically active islands near the Antarctic. A volcanic eruption on McDonald Island in 1992 was the first there in 75,000 years. Since 1992, the island has doubled in size due to the volcanic activity.
- Penguins and seals use the islands as breeding sites.
- Heard Island glaciers are used by climate scientists to study climate change.

Management of the Heritage Site

- The islands are managed as reserves.
- All visits for any purpose are strictly controlled.
- Commercial fishing is not permitted within the heritage site boundary.
- Quarantine regulations stop the introduction of pests and weeds.
- Australian Defence Force vessels patrol the area, looking for any illegal fishing or landings on the islands.

How Do Scientists Survive When They Visit?

Due to its dangerous coastline, McDonald Island is very difficult to reach by sea. Scientists can visit the more accessible Heard Island, but it still takes around ten days or more to get there by sea, through the roughest waters in the world. Researchers who study the islands usually stay for a few weeks, living in tents or huts. They use diesel generators, solar cells and wind power to provide their electricity. Rubbish is returned to Australia when they leave.

Glossary

aesthetic	relating to beauty
heritage	thing or characteristic that is handed down from previous generations
mantle rocks	Earth's rock layer between the hot inner core and the outer, thin crust
mortar	used to cement stones or bricks together in a building
rehabilitate	return to a previous and better condition
species	separate group of animals or plants
tectonic plate	huge masses of land that move across the Earth at a very slow pace
transportation	sending convicts from Britain to the Australian colonies
UNESCO	United Nations Educational, Scientific and Cultural Organization

---

Index

Visit these websites to find out more about Australia's World Heritage Sites and special places

whc.unesco.org/en/list
www.environment.gov.au/heritage